THANKSGIVING
PROGRAM BUILDER
No. 2

Program Ideas for All Ages

Recitations—Poems—Readings
Plays—Songs

Compiled by Evelyn Stenbock

Permission to make photocopies of program builders
is granted to the purchaser
when three books have been purchased.
The photocopies cannot be sold, loaned, or given away.

Copyright © 1981 by Lillenas Publishing Co.
All Rights Reserved.   Litho in U.S.A.

GRADED PROGRAM MATERIAL

Ages 3-5

Gracious Greeter

I'm the gracious greeter
   Selected for this day;
Welcome, and Happy Thanksgiving
   Is all I have to say!

—*Helen Kitchell Evans*

Little Mother

(For a child and her small brother who go hand in hand to platform.)

I'm glad for my little brother.
Jesus said, "Love one another."
(Puts arm around little brother.)

—*Velda Blumhagen*

We Give Thanks

(Exercise for 12 little tots. Staple the letters "WE GIVE THANKS" to headbands. Each child says one line.)

  W-e can walk

  E-ach can talk

  G-ive our thanks to God.

  I-n His care

  V-ery safely there

  E-veryone gives thanks to God.

  T-ogether we run

  H-ave lots of fun

  A-nd we give our thanks to God.

  N-ow in our way

  K-indly we say,

  S-o always give thanks to God!

—*Helen Kitchell Evans*

Why Me?

I'm a thankful little child.
   Why me? Why me?
Because I'm loved very much
   By a great big family!

—*Helen Kitchell Evans*

Little for Sure

I'm a little tot for sure
   But big enough to say
I'm thankful for Jesus
   On this Thanksgiving Day.

—*Helen Kitchell Evans*

We Thank Thee

For tiny seeds,
   For drops of rain,
For sunshine
   That brings harvest grain,
     We thank Thee!

For love at home,
   For love each day
From friends we know,
   With whom we play,
     We thank Thee!

For all good things
   That come our way;
For freedom where
   Each one can play,
     We thank Thee!

For Thanksgiving Day,
   For family, too,
Dear God, we're thankful,
   And grateful to You!
     We thank Thee!

—*Helen Kitchell Evans*

Thank You, God

(An exercise for three children)

1st Child *(while all fold hands):*
We'll fold our hands,

2nd Child *(while all bow heads):*
We'll bow our heads,

3rd Child *(holds up head):*
And this is what we pray:

Unison *(all in attitude of prayer):*
Thank You, God,
For love and care
This glad Thanksgiving Day.
—Velda Blumhagen

Thank You, God

For a nose to smell
   The flowers sweet,
And a tongue to taste
   The food I eat—
Thank You, God, for these.

For ears to hear
   And eyes to see
The beautiful world
   God planned to be—
Thank You, God, for these!

For hands to touch
   And use each day,
For feet to run
   And jump and play—
Thank You, God, for these.

For sunshine bright,
   For raindrops, too,
For nighttime rest
   When day is through—
Thank You, God, for these!

For Your great love
   And forgiveness, too.
For Your care for me
   Whatever I do—
Thank You, God, for these!
—Merle Glasgow

Jesus Said

Jesus said, "Come unto me,"
And so I'm glad to say
That we can bid you welcome
On this Thanksgiving Day.
—Mildred L. Wills

So Many Things

I have so many things
   To thank God for each day:
My family, home, and church,
   And friends with whom I play.

But most of all I thank Him for
   His kind and loving care,
And because I know He loves me—
   He is with me everywhere!
—Merle Glasgow

Happy Pilgrims

(An exercise for four small children dressed as Pilgrims.)

1st Child *(carries hymnbook)*—
We are happy Pilgrims
   Marching on our way;
Going to the Meeting House
   This Thanksgiving Day.

2nd Child *(carries toy gun)*—
Mother carries Bible,
   Father carries gun.
   (crouches low, clutching gun)
We must watch for enemies;
   We can make them run!

3rd Child *(carries Bible)*—
Then we sit down quietly,
   Listen to God's Word,
Hear the story of Jesus,
   Sweetest ever heard.

4th Child *(carries pumpkin)*—
When the meeting's over,
   Home we go to dine.
What a happy day we have
   At Thanksgiving time!
—Mildred L. Wills

Welcome

Surely I'm a tiny one,
  To welcome you and say,
"We're glad to have you with us
  This glad Thanksgiving Day!"
—*Mildred L. Wills*

It's Good to Set a Day Apart

It's good to set a day apart
And thank our Father from the heart
For the gifts of love His mercy sends,
And His love and care that never ends.
—*Margaret N. Freeman*

I'm Thankful

I'm thankful for my mother's love;
  I'm thankful for my dad.
I'm thankful for the Lord above
  Who keeps me ever glad.
—*Samuel H. Cox*

This Special Day

I'm not so big; I am quite small.
You might think I've no thanks at all
To give to God this special day,
But listen now to what I say.

Though I'm so small, I'm thankful, too,
For Mom and Dad and friends like you.
I hope they'll always thankful be
They had a little child like me.
—*Eleanor Pankow*

I'm Big Enough to Say

I'm little, I know, to be standing here,
  But I'm big enough to say:
I've got a big place in my heart for God
  Full of thankfulness today!
—*Margaret N. Freeman*

Each Day

Each day we must live for Jesus
  And be thankful for everything,
Not just set one day aside
  For thanks to the Heavenly King.
—*Helen Kitchell Evans*

Little Pilgrims

Little Pilgrims must have been
  Very, very good
On that first Thanksgiving Day
  In the deep, dark wood.

Though the winter had been hard,
  Very, very long,
Summer came to them at last
  Filled with sweet birdsong.

Now Thanksgiving Day had dawned,
  Very, very bright.
Little Pilgrims bowed in prayer.
  What a thankful sight!
—*Dorothy Wills Jenks*

GRADED PROGRAM MATERIAL

Ages 6-8

Extra Hugs

Grandmother hugs me closely,
  Grandpa says, "You're a dear."
I get a lot of extra hugs
  When Thanksgiving Day is here!

—Helen Kitchell Evans

What It Stands For

T stands for *Thanksgiving*
  That comes to us each fall.

H is for our *hearts*
  Filled with love for all.

A is for *affection*
  We have for all our friends.

N is used for *never*,
  Because it never ends.

K we use for *kindness*
  We show to everyone.

S is for *salvation;*
  The gift of God's own Son.

G is for our *gratitude,*
  And grateful we should be.

I for *interesting days*
  With all our family.

V is for *variety*
  In all our family fun.

I is for *ideas*
  Shared by everyone.

N is for the *nation*
  Where we are proud to be.

G is for *God's goodness*
  In our land of liberty!

—Helen Kitchell Evans

All Our Days

Grateful hearts now sing
Praise to Christ our King,
For His wondrous love
And for heaven above.

Some day we shall be
There, eternally.
But, till then, we'll praise
Jesus all our days.

—Samuel H. Cox

Why We're Here

UNISON—
We're standing here today
Because we're thankful:

1ST BOY—
For nice wooly mittens,

1ST GIRL—
For soft fluffy kittens,

2ND BOY—
For birds in the trees,

2ND GIRL—
For soft autumn breeze,

3RD BOY—
For rain and for snow—

3RD GIRL—
On and on we could go!

UNISON—
We'll just stop and say
We're so thankful today!

—Helen Kitchell Evans

Thankful

(An exercise for three children)

1st Child—
Thankful for the sunshine;
  Thankful for the rain;
Thankful for the harvest fields
  Ripe with golden grain.

2nd Child—
Thankful for my mother;
  Thankful for my dad;
Thankful for the kindest folks
  A fellow [girl] ever had!

3rd Child—
Thankful for our Sunday School;
  Thankful for God's Word;
But most of all we're thankful
  That Jesus is our Lord!

—Dorothy W. Jenks

A Thanksgiving

Thank You, dear God,
  For eyes to see
The beauty in
  Both sky and tree.

Thank You, dear God,
  For ears to hear
Tidings rich
  With joy and cheer.

Thank You, dear God,
  For tongue to praise
The wonders of
  Thy loving ways.

Thank You, dear God,
  For hands to use
In doing all
  The good I choose.

Thank You, dear God,
  For feet to tread
The narrow path
  So straight ahead.

—Lucille Clarke

Everybody Should

I'm thankful for my family;
  I'm thankful for my friends;
I'm thankful for my Savior
  Who my every need attends.

I thank Him for these blessings
  And for everything that's good.
I thank Him, 'cause I love Him,
  Just as everybody should.

—Samuel H. Cox

With Thankful Hearts

(An exercise for several children, each holding an open Bible in his hand. If convenient there should be some kind of "horn of plenty" on the platform containing apples, grapes, partly husked corn, potatoes, etc. This number is best at the close of the program.)

Children in Unison—
"O give thanks unto the Lord, for he is good."

(Children close their Bibles.)
This special time we want to say
How glad we are you came today.
Let's join all nature as we bring
Our thank-yous to the blessed King.

And now with gladness let us lift
Our hearts in love for every gift.
And God who made us, will rejoice
To see each child and hear each voice.

(The children sing some song of thankfulness such as "Praise Him, Praise Him," after which the leader or teacher of the group prays a prayer of thanksgiving.)

Children in Unison—
Our worship service now is through
But songs of praise will stay with you.
For home and friends and sun and air,
Let's think our thank-yous everywhere.

—Flora E. Breck

We Are Thankful

(An exercise for six children)

1st Child—
I'm smiling, as you all can see
Because I am so glad to be
Right here to take my place and say,
"God bless each one, in every way."

2nd Child—
I'm happy, too. I am so glad
To have the world's best mom and dad;
They care for me and teach me, too,
The things I should and shouldn't do.

3rd Child—
I'm thankful for the chance to run,
And fish, and swim, and have such fun;
But now it's getting colder, so
We'll soon play in the drifted snow.

4th Child—
I like to come to Sunday School
For here I learned the golden rule;
I love my teacher, for she tries
To help me to be good and wise.

5th Child—
I'm happy, too, for on this day
We meet at church to sing and pray;
Our pastor reads God's Holy Word,
The sweetest story ever heard.

6th Child—
We're thankful for so many things—
The peace and joy salvation brings
And that we live where we are free
To worship God in liberty.

Unison *(with heads bowed and eyes closed)*—
We ask Thee, Lord, to bless each one
  Who's gathered with us here today,
And may our hearts in gratitude
  Bring others to Thy way. Amen.

—*Dorothy Conant Stroud*

We Give Thanks

(An exercise for a class of children)

1st Child—
For our home and parents, too,
For loving care the whole year
  through,

Unison—
We give thanks unto Thee, O God.

2nd Child—
For our food and clothes to wear,
For enough that we can share,

Unison—
We give thanks unto Thee, O God.

3rd Child—
For our church friends far and near,
For God's children far and near,

Unison—
It is a good thing to give thanks to the
  Lord.

—*Velda Blumhagen*

Thanksgiving Psalm

God gives us gifts
  So we should share
With other children
  Everywhere.

God sends us joy
  So we should sing
In gratitude
  For everything.

God keeps us safe
  So we should know
He rules the skies
  And earth below.

God fills our needs
  So we should give
Thanks to Him
  Each day we live.

—*Lucille Clarke*

When First the Pilgrims Came

Our country was a woodland
   When first the Pilgrims came—
A very, very good land
   For which they praised God's name.
And now, with ev'ry city
   We have that highly ranks,
'Twould be an awful pity
   If we did not give thanks.

—Vida Munden Nixon

Hear Ye! Hear Ye!

(Child dressed as town crier enters from rear of auditorium ringing bell, saying, "Hear Ye!")

Many, many years ago
   A man dressed much like me
Rang a bell and cried the news—
   No TV then to see!

"Hear ye! Hear ye!" loud he called,
   Then he rang the bell;
"Hear ye! Hear ye! Hear ye!
   I have news to tell."

I'm not an old town crier,
   But I came here to cry,
"Thanksgiving Day is coming!
   Don't let it pass you by!"

—Helen Kitchell Evans

Truly Great

(Children carry a flag)

1st CHILD—
Here's a banner of Thanksgiving
   For all of you to see;
We're very proud to carry it
   For it stands for liberty.

2nd CHILD—
We're thankful for our country,
   Our nation is really grand!
Here righteousness is honored
   In a truly Christian land!

—Helen Kitchell Evans

Thank You

(A Prayer)

Thank You, dear God,
For all good gifts;
   We know they come from You—
The food we eat,
The clothes we wear,
   Our homes and churches, too.

Thank You for
Our families
   And for love that we can share;
Thank You, God,
Because Your love
   Is for people everywhere.
      Amen.

—Merle Glasgow

Our Thanks

(For nine children who display large cutout letters.)

1st CHILD:
O—"O give thanks unto the Lord, for he is good." (Psalm 107:1a)

2nd CHILD:
U—"Unto thee, O Lord, do I lift up my soul." (Psalm 25:1)

3rd CHILD:
R—"Rejoice and be exceeding glad: for great is your reward in heaven." (Matthew 5:12a)

4th CHILD:
T—"The earth is the Lord's, and the fulness thereof." (Psalm 24:1a)

5th CHILD:
H—"... happy is that people, whose God is the Lord." (Psalm 144:15b)

6th CHILD:
A—"And God saw every thing that he had made, and, behold, it was very good." (Genesis 1:31a)

7TH CHILD:
N—"... now are we the sons of God, and it doth not yet appear what we shall be." (1 John 3:2a)

8TH CHILD:
K—"Know ye that the Lord he is God: it is he that hath made us." (Psalm 100:3a)

9TH CHILD:
S—"... seek, and ye shall find; knock, and it shall be opened unto you." (Matthew 7:7b)

UNISON:
Our thanks to God
We bring this day.
In love we'll try
To live His way.

—Velda Blumhagen

A Big Hello

(Print the word "Hello" on a roll of white paper. After the children recite the verses, they should unroll it and shout "Hello!")

1ST CHILD—
I'm thankful for my mom and dad
And all my family.
I love each one so very much,
They mean the world to me.

2ND CHILD—
I'm thankful for my church today,
And all my friends so dear.
I'm thankful this Thanksgiving time
That all of you are here!

UNISON—
Yes, we are thankful children;
We know you're thankful, too.
We want to bid you welcome—
Here's a big HELLO for you!

—Helen Kitchell Evans

Thank You, Jesus

(For 12 children each, with one line and one letter, or 6 children with two lines and two letters each.)

T is for the many thanks
   I give to God this day,

H is for the many blessings
   He gives along the way.

A is for another day
   In which to give Him praise,

N is for the new life
   He gives that lasts always.

K is for His kindness as
   He guides me in all I do,

S is because He shows me
   His love so good and true.

G is because He gives me
   A thankful song to sing,

I is because I love Him
   A thankful heart *I* bring.

V is for my voice
   to tell others about Him,

I is because I'm thankful
   I let the Savior in.

N is for my Savior,
   my never-failing friend,

G is for my God and King
   who'll be with me to the end.

ALL—So, thank You, thank You, Jesus,
And may this Thanksgiving Day,
Be only the start of a thankful heart
For each and every day.

—Carolyn R. Scheidies

GRADED PROGRAM MATERIAL

Ages 9-11

Thanksgiving

The Pilgrims set a day apart
   So all mankind could bring
Their thanks to God for blessing them
   With every goodly thing.

And so today we follow them
   And from our hearts make known
Our gratitude for all the love
   Our God to us has shown.

            —*Lucille Clarke*

Our Gratitude

(An exercise for four children)

1st Child—

Our fathers from across the sea
Came here to find true liberty;
From east to west they made a way
For us to live so well today.

2nd Child—

They cleared the forests, tilled the soil,
And all their days were filled with toil
Except the Sabbath, when they met.
(Their God they never would forget.)

3rd Child—

And now, today, we gather here
To give thanks for another year
Of golden sunshine, summer rain,
And autumn fields of golden grain.

4th Child—

As we assemble here today
To thank God for His faithful way,
Our words can only half express
Our gratitude and happiness.

         —*Dorothy Conant Stroud*

Share

When summer's gone
And nature dons
   A colorful array
Of crisping leaves
On sleepy trees
   Then we begin to say:

"The Lord is good,"
And so we should
   Be thankful for His care
In giving us,
Providing us,
   With plenty left to share.

So let us praise
And glad hearts raise
   Our thanks to God above.
Let's share our joys
With girls and boys
   Who know not of God's love.

           —*Samuel H. Cox*

Thankful

We have many, many things
   For which we wish to say,
"Thank You, dear Lord Jesus,"
   On Thanksgiving Day.

Thank You, Heavenly Father,
   For Your loving care;
For health and home and parents—
   Your love is everywhere!

Let us join our voices
   In a hymn of praise.
Let us follow Jesus;
   Let us learn His ways.

           —*Mildred L. Wills*

In All Our Ways

All the family has come—
  Grandpa, Grandma, cousins, too;
Eagerly they ask, "Well, how
  Has the world been treating you?"

The table then is spread with food—
  Turkey, brown and steaming hot;
Gravy, sauces, pickles, pie—
  Can't quite think what there is not.

Then we pause and bow our heads,
  And our hearts near burst with praise
For the tender way our Lord
  Blesses us in all our ways.

—*Dorothy Conant Stroud*

Happy Days

(An exercise for two boys and two girls)

1st GIRL *(points to boy on her right)*—
The happy days of long ago
  That some folks talk about,
Are days that you and I today
  Will have to do without.

1st BOY *(dressed as cowboy)*—
The wagon trains, the spinning wheels,
  The one-horse open sleigh,
The cowboys fighting Indians
  Today are out of the fray.

2nd BOY *(dressed as policeman or just wearing a toy badge)*—
The happy days we live today
  Are happier because
Each color, creed, and race receives
  Protection from our laws.
(Points to his badge.)

2nd GIRL *(carrying U.S. flag at side)*—
We thank God for our land so great,
  Our land of liberty.
(Holds flag high.)
A haven for the homeless who
  Are striving to be free.

—*Samuel H. Cox*

A Child's Thanksgiving Prayer

For parents and their love and care
And all the happy things they share,
  Father, we thank Thee.

For clothes and warmth and drink and food
And all that makes our life so good,
  Father, we thank Thee.

For the big, round sun shining bright
And sky and moon and star at night,
  Father, we thank Thee.

For grasses, flowers, and tall trees,
For squirrels and rabbits, birds and bees,
  Father, we thank Thee.

For the church house majestically tall
Which gives to us our Father's call,
  Father, we thank Thee.

—*Ruth Vaughn*

We Thank Thee for So Many Things

We thank Thee, Lord, for all we have,
  And, oh, we give Thee praise
For loving care, for needs supplied,
  And lovely sunlit days.

We thank Thee for our many friends,
  And parents kind and true,
For teachers in our Sunday School,
  And for our preacher, too.

We thank Thee for so many things,
  And that our Jesus came
To save us from our every sin
  By taking all our blame.

We want to thank Thee once again
  And ask that Thou wilt go
With everyone who's gathered here,
  That they Thy love may know.

—*Dorothy Conant Stroud*

My Thanksgiving Prayer

I thank God for taking care of me
   Each and every day;
For guiding my footsteps
   And listening when I pray.

I thank God for taking care of me
   The whole year through;
For helping me in all
   That I say and do.

I hope I haven't left anything out
   Because you see
I want to thank God
   For everything He's done for me.

—*Beverly Ann Hoffeditz*

The Giver

(An exercise for two children)

1st Child—
I'm glad God made this land of ours
   So wonderful with all
The shining rivers, lakes, and rills,
   And mountains, snowcapped, high.
I'm glad He made the rolling hills
   And valleys green below
Where in the springtime violets
   And bright wild flowers grow.

2nd Child—
I'm glad for fields of golden grain
   That stretch for mile on mile,
And for the shaded roadside nooks
   That bid us rest awhile.
I'm glad for lovely birds that sing,
   And puppies at their play;
For brilliant sunsets in the west
   As evening follows day.

Unison—
There are so many, many things
   We should be thankful for;
And, oh, the Giver of all these
   Our grateful hearts adore.

—*Dorothy Conant Stroud*

A Thanksgiving Prayer

(An exercise for three children)

1st Child—
Lord, help us to be thankful,
   Help us to be free.
Set our feet on higher ground
   To better live for Thee.

2nd Child—
Lord, help us to be thoughtful,
   Help us to be kind.
Help us to be merciful
   That we may mercy find.

3rd Child—
Lord, help us to be pure in heart,
   And bless the path we've trod,
That we may ever faithful be
   And someday see our God!

—*Mildred L. Wills*

Every Day I Live

The food we eat, the clothes we wear,
Our feet that take us everywhere,
Our hands that hold, that work and do
The many things we want them to;

Our homes, so cozy and so wide,
So comforting to get inside;
Our parents, strong and true and
   good,
Training us the way they should—

For all these things and many more,
My Lord I gratefully adore.
To Him, my life I gladly give
And thank Him every day I live.

—*Samuel H. Cox*

We Give Him Our Most Grateful Praise

(An exercise for six children)

1st Child—
I'm thankful for
  So many things—
For birds that wheel
  On flashing wings,
For trees, now bare,
  But lovely still;
Against the sky
  My heart they thrill.

2nd Child—
I'm thankful for
  The golden grain,
For spring-warm sun
  And summer rain,
For rolling plains
  And mountains high,
And brooks that laugh
  As they rush by.

3rd Child—
I'm thankful for
  The food we need,
Which God makes grow
  From tiny seed;
I'm thankful that
  He will provide
Necessities,
  And more beside.

4th Child—
I'm thankful for
  Our church so dear,
And for our friends
  Who worship here;
God blesses us
  In every way
As we meet here
  This lovely day.

5th Child—
I'm thankful that
  Our country's free
And that we live
  In liberty;
Without a fear
  Our Lord we praise,
And joyfully
  Our voices raise.

6th Child—
For nature, food, and
  Parents dear,
For all the things
  God gives us here,
We give Him our
  Most grateful praise
And gladly walk
  In His dear ways.

Unison—
(All sing, "Praise Him! Praise Him.")

—*Dorothy Conant Stroud*

My Family

There is a mother at our house who is special as can be;
She cares for all the little folks and loves them tenderly.

There is a dad at our house who follows Jesus' way;
He fixes things and does his work and guards us all the way.

There is a sister at our house, so cute and warm and sweet;
When it comes to little sisters, she just can't be beat.

There is a brother at our house, a nuisance and a pest,
But I have to own I love him, just like all the rest.

I have a prayer for my house, now Thanksgiving is here:
Thank You, God, for those we love; please bless them all the year.

—*Myrtle E. Felkner*

The Best Gift

A Skit for 11 Children

by Velda Blumhagen

The scene takes place in a church school classroom. A table is at center of platform. Chairs are around the table. There are 11 characters taking part: a narrator, a teacher and four other girls, and five boys.

The Skit

Narrator—The children of the Doers of the Word class are about to bring gifts to fill a Thanksgiving basket for an elderly man of their church. Mr. Wilson lives alone and is very poor. The children were asked to use their own money to buy food or to make things to use as gifts.

The scene takes place in their church classroom. Miss Duncan, the teacher, enters platform and places a basket in the center of the table. She then sits at the head of the table, opens her Bible and starts to read.

Miss Duncan *(as Ruth enters carrying wrapped loaves of bread)*—Hello, Ruth. You're the first one to bring something for our Thanksgiving basket.

Ruth—I brought loaves of bread my mother helped me bake. I had never made bread before, but she showed me how. I think it turned out real good. I used my allowance money to buy the flour and yeast.

Ellen *(entering platform carrying a bag of cookies)*—I brought cookies I made. I paid for the materials I used, too. I made the cookies all by myself!

Miss Duncan *(placing bread and cookies in basket)*—M-m-m-m-m-m! Smells good!

John *(as he and Cecil enter and place cans of fruit and vegetables on table)*—We bought canned things at the store. Mr. Wilson can eat this anytime.

Cecil—We used our allowance money for this week.

Emily *(enters with Jane carrying bags of oranges and grapefruit)*—I earned money baby-sitting to buy these oranges.

Jane—Saturday, Mother paid me extra for helping clean the basement. I used the money to buy these grapefruit for Mr. Wilson.

Miss Duncan *(putting food into the basket)*—These are all good, thoughtful gifts.

Jack *(enters carrying a box of raisins)*—I couldn't spare any of my allowance money because I'm buying the skates I didn't get for my birthday. My grandmother sent me a box of raisins along with her gift of cookies and candies. I don't like raisins. Mr. Wilson can have them. *(Tosses box on table.)*

Jane—What if Mr. Wilson doesn't like raisins either? Mom said I should get something easy to chew.

Emily—Jack just didn't want to spend his money on someone else. He wants it all for himself.

Jack *(sarcastically)*—So what!

Miss Duncan—Now, boys and girls, let's remember to keep the Christian spirit in all our giving. We must not judge why Jack gave the raisins.

Stephen *(enters empty-handed, looking at basket)*—Oh, I forgot all about that basket and I've spent all of this week's allowance. I wanted a new horn for my bicycle.

Ruth *(under her breath)*—Lame excuse, I'd say.

Miss Duncan—Jerry isn't here yet, but we can start looking up our new class motto verse. *(Gives Bibles to Emily to pass out.)*

Jerry *(enters with a white slip of paper in his hand)*—I'm sorry to be late. I had to help Mother get Grandfather into his wheelchair. Then I had to bring breakfast to him. He wanted me to get all sorts of things for him.

Miss Duncan—You were being helpful, anyway.

Jerry *(handing note paper to Miss Duncan)*—I don't have a father to give me an allowance. Mom can't spare any out of what she makes. I brought a promise gift.

Miss Duncan *(taking note and reading it aloud)*—"Dear Mr. Wilson: I will sweep your walks and shovel the snow whenever needed. I will do these things for you free. It's my Thanksgiving gift. Jerry."

Miss Duncan *(turning to Jerry)*—That's a very thoughtful gift that will last all winter. Mr. Wilson has rheumatism and I know he'll appreciate this.

Stephen—I'm sorry I forgot. I'm sorry my money is all spent. Could I write another promise gift to put in the basket? I go by Mr. Wilson's house on my way to school. I could mail his letters and bring his paper home. I'd like to offer to be his errand boy.

Several Class Members—That's a good present, Stephen!

Miss Duncan—This basket should really make Mr. Wilson happy. And remember, boys and girls, the best gift of all is the gift of friendship. Let us not forget our shut-in friend all through the year. Now, let's put our card on top of the basket. *(Shows card and reads.)*

"Happy Thanksgiving
from
Doers of the Word Class"

Shall we read our new motto verse and try to memorize it?

Unison—". . . be ye doers of the word, and not hearers only . . ."

GRADED PROGRAM MATERIAL | **Junior High**

A Conversation

(An exercise for Junior High)

By Helen Kitchell Evans

1st Child—We *should* be thankful for everything we have!

2nd Child—But you just said Thanksgiving Day *wasn't* just for being thankful for things we have!

1st Child—That what I said, and that's what I meant.

3rd Child—I don't get it. What do you mean?

1st Child—Everyone stands around being so thankful for all they have and all they get, but . . .

4th Child—You mean you think Thanksgiving is for something else, too?

1st Child—Yes, I most certainly do!

5th Child—Well, fill us in. We seem to be in the dark about what you are trying to tell us.

6th Child—Oh, I get it! I'm thankful I can help my mother by looking after my baby brother!

1st Child—That's it!

4th Child—I'm thankful I can cut the grass and shovel snow, and let my father rest.

5th Child—I'm thankful I can use my bike to run errands.

1st Child—That's it. Now you all have the right idea! How about you, _____?

2nd Child—I guess I'm thankful I can go shopping for my neighbor, who's crippled.

7th Child—You know, I never thought of Thanksgiving in this way!

2nd Child—Me either! But it sure does make me feel good. Let's all go do something good for other people this Thanksgiving!

Bring Thanks Today

Let all the earth
    Bring thanks today
For blessings that
    Have come our way.

Let everyone
    Be still and know
From whence these gifts
    So richly flow.

Let gratitude
    And pure love bind
The hearts and hands
    Of all mankind.

      —Lucille Clarke

Thank You, God

1st Child—

Thank You most of all for Jesus
    Who saves us all from sin.
Thank You for the Holy Spirit
    Who gives us peace within.

2nd Child—

Thank You for the church and
    preachers,
And missionaries too.
Thank You for Your Word, the Bible,
    That tells us what to do.

3rd Child—

Thank You for our homes and families
    And friends and loved ones dear.
Thanks for all the daily blessings
    And thanks for being near.

4th Child—

Thanks for hearing all our prayers
    And thank You for answering, too.
Thanks for love and strength and
    courage.
Our Father above, thank You.

Unison—
Amen.

      —Patricia Ulery

Not Just on Thanksgiving

We're thankful for our parents—
    To us they're very dear;
We're thankful for our Savior
    Who is always near.

Not just on Thanksgiving
    But every single day,
We must count our blessings
    As God shows us the way.

(Memorize and repeat 1 Thessalonians 5:18.)

      —Helen Kitchell Evans

We Have Thanksgiving Day

There is food upon the table
    And our hearts are filled with cheer.
All are very thankful
    When Thanksgiving Day is here.

With our grateful hearts this day
    We praise our Savior up above
And thank Him for His blessings
    And everlasting love.

On the last of each November
    We praise our God and pray.
We are very, very thankful
    So we have Thanksgiving Day.

      —Helen Kitchell Evans

Why We Are Grateful

Why are we grateful
    And why do we sing?
Why are we happy
    And thanksgiving bring?

Why do we know
    Every need will be met
With blessings unnumbered
    In store for us yet?

Because there's a God
    Who in earth and above
Reigns over all
    With wisdom and love.

      —Lucille Clarke

Thanksgiving

The crops have now been gathered in
   And there is food for all.
Oh, may we share the good things
   Of harvest time in fall;

That all the people of the world
   May have their daily bread.
We show our thanks to God
   When the needy ones are fed.

The church bell rings again for us
   On this Thanksgiving Day.
May we help to send God's blessings
   To all along our way.

          —Velda Blumhagen

What Is Thanksgiving?

SOLO—
What is Thanksgiving?

CHORUS—
It's cold, gray skies
   And a brownish hue
On fields where once
   A harvest grew.

SOLO 2—
What is Thanksgiving?

CHORUS—
It's pumpkin pie
   And smells of spice
That makes Thanksgiving
   Day so nice.

SOLO 3—
What is Thanksgiving?

CHORUS—
It's festive hours
   With family,
And relatives
   We seldom see!

SOLO 1—
What is Thanksgiving?

SOLO 2—
Most of all
   It's time to pray,
Giving thanks to God
   For our good way.

CHORUS—
For Christian friends
   And a happy life.
That's Thanksgiving!

          —Helen Kitchell Evans

What It Means

Thanksgiving just means giving thanks
   To Jesus up above *(points upward)*
For all the blessings that He gives,
   For all His care and love.

Thanksgiving just means giving thanks
   From way down deep inside.
(Places hand over heart.)
A thankful heart invites the Lord
   To enter and abide.

          —Dorothy Wills Jenks

Thank You for the Fall

(Exercise for seven children)

UNISON—Sing a song of autumn,

1ST CHILD—Apples in the bin,

2ND CHILD—Pumpkins in the garden,

3RD CHILD—Corn all gatherin' in.

UNISON—Sing a song of autumn,

4TH CHILD—Look at each lovely tree,

5TH CHILD—Yellow, red, and golden,

6TH CHILD—Brilliant as can be.

UNISON—Sing a song of autumn:

7TH CHILD—Food enough for all.

UNISON—Thank You, God, who gave us
   The *beautiful, beautiful* fall!

          —Helen Kitchell Evans

Because We're Grateful

Because we are so grateful,
    Dear Lord, we come today
To thank You for the glorious gifts
    You daily send our way.

We thank You for Your loving care
    And lovely days of spring;
For flowered lanes alive with bees
    And sight of birds awing.

We thank You for the dew and rain
    And church bells as they ring;
With thankful hearts we want to say,
    "Thank You for everything."

—Lucille Clarke

Thanksgiving Every Day

Thanksgiving is on the calendar
    As but one thoughtful day,
Reminding us to praise the Lord
    And thank Him when we pray.

But this is not suggesting
    That other days should be
A time of *not* remembering
    God's kindnesses to me!

Make every day Thanksgiving!
    Let's praise Him as we pray;
And let us show our gratitude
    In all we do and say!

—E. L. Russell

Song of Thanksgiving

Choral Reading from Psalms 75 and 100

Reading Divisions—
    Narrator
    Group One
    Group Two

Unison—Unto thee, O God, do we give thanks, unto thee do we give thanks:

Narrator—Make a joyful noise unto the Lord, all ye lands.

Group One—Serve the Lord with gladness:

Group Two—come before his presence with singing.

Narrator—Know ye that the Lord he is God:

Group Two—it is he that hath made us, and not we ourselves;

Group One—we are his people, and the sheep of his pasture.

Narrator—Enter into his gates with thanksgiving, and into his courts with praise:

Group One—be thankful unto him, and bless his name. For the Lord is good;

Group Two—his mercy is everlasting;

Unison—and his truth endureth to all generations.

—Arranged by Carolyn R. Scheidies

GRADED PROGRAM MATERIAL

Senior High and Adult

Being Grateful

Wasted hours and wasted days
Without a time of giving praise.
Wasted effort is the word
Unless encouragement is heard.

Lives are wasted, thrown away
Unless we're thankful when we pray.
Every gift from God is good
Let us live with gratitude.

—*E. L. Russell*

To Be Thankful

Oh, with thankful hearts to gaze
  On this universe of God;
To see the guidance of His hand
  Where weary feet have trod.

Oh, with thankful hearts to see
  The wonders of His love;
The singing birds, the blooming
    flow'rs;
  The clouds and skies above.

Oh, with thankful hearts to hear
  The reading of His Word;
To know that through the passing
    years,
  His gentle voice is heard.

Oh, with thankful hearts to give
  Of what God does bestow.
As holders of these bounteous gifts—
  God's stewards here below.

—*Mildred L. Wills*

Thanksgiving Psalm

Because He's God
He clothes the earth with green,
And woods and hills rejoice!
Because He's God
The mountains stay or move
Whichever way He chooses
When He lifts up His voice.
And water stays or falls
In drops of rain
To soften every furrow
Of the plowman
And sheaves of golden grain
Clothe hills and fields.
God makes the night and morning.
To rejoice
When He lifts up His voice!
So make a joyful noise unto the Lord!
All creatures in Him living
Praise Him now
And bring your vow—
Your vow of loud thanksgiving!

—*Ethel V. Leffel*

Don't Take the Lord for Granted

Don't take the Lord for granted
  Although His gifts are free;
For every good gift is from Him
  Who blesses abundantly.

We humans like a word of thanks
  For kindnesses we share,
So let's say thank You to our God
  For all His love and care.

—*E. L. Russell*

The "Thank You" Habit

A skit for a Women's November Meeting

By Ethel V. Leffel

Characters—
  The hostess
  The guests, including one leader

Scene—
  A living room. The ladies have been doing missionary sewing and are about to take a coffee break.

LEADER—Thanksgiving next week. I suppose you all have your dinners planned. Do you know, I was just sitting here thinking—aren't we lucky to be sitting in this nice warm home, eating this beautiful food that ——— fixed just for us? And just look at her pretty dishes! We have it so good, don't we? Thanksgiving should have a special meaning to all of us. We have so much to be thankful for!

HOSTESS *(filling coffee cups)*—Maybe we have too much. It's quite different from the first Thanksgiving, isn't it? Theirs really had to be an outpouring of thankfulness to God from truly grateful hearts. Maybe we have it too good to be that thankful.

1ST SPEAKER—Yes, God has really blessed us. I'm glad we have time and money to make these baby quilts and mittens for people who don't have it as good as we do. It's a real privilege to do these things. It's the least we can do.

2ND SPEAKER—Isn't it good to be in such a thankful mood? But I'm ashamed to say that we have to get into the mood to be thankful!

3RD SPEAKER—That's true. Thanksgiving should be an everyday thing. It should be as much a part of talking to God as asking for things.

4TH SPEAKER—It's easy to be thankful when we have it good. But could we be thankful if we lost our material things; our cars, our homes, our food supply?

LEADER—You know, I really didn't mean to get us into such a somber discussion.

HOSTESS—No, no, Mary! I think this is good for us.

1ST SPEAKER—I do, too. Did you know that the prophet Habakkuk gives us a lesson in thanking God when things go wrong? *(Turns in her Bible to Habakkuk 3:17-18, NIV.)* Listen *(reads)*: "Though the fig tree does not bud and there are no grapes on the vines, though the olive crop fails and the fields produce no food, though there are no sheep in the pen and no cattle in the stalls, yet I will rejoice in the Lord, I will be joyful in God my Savior."

If we could just think in this vein! We have gotten so much from God—our very lives, our salvation through Christ—that God deserves our thanks even when our physical bodies aren't so comfortable.

2ND SPEAKER—I remember once when I was a child, we had meat loaf for our Thanksgiving dinner. I was ashamed to tell anyone what we had. I wanted turkey. I didn't feel a bit thankful!

3RD SPEAKER—You were just a child and didn't understand. We need to be sure as adults that we don't have a childish view. We need to develop hearts that praise God for who He is and what He has done to meet our spiritual needs rather than what He gives us of material blessings. Not that we shouldn't appreciate them, too. Our thanks should just go a little deeper than surface things.

4TH SPEAKER—I remember a missionary to Rhodesia telling about one of their Rhodesian converts who had a truly thankful heart. She was a little old lady who lived alone in a little hut out in the woods. By our standards, she was destitute. And yet whenever they came to call on her, she would be praising and thanking God. She had a heart of praise, not forced, but a heart that couldn't help thanking God.

5TH SPEAKER—Doesn't it make us feel ungrateful? Do you remember when Jesus healed the 10 lepers? Only one returned to thank Him. Do you remember what He said? "Were there not 10? Where are the other 9?" I believe that their ingratitude really grieved His heart.

6TH SPEAKER—Yes, and in the first chapter of Romans you remember that God condemned the people because they were unthankful! In fact, it was the first step on a downward course away from God. Read it when you get time. The whole chapter. It really speaks to the heart!

HOSTESS *(passing the cookies)*—Do you know I've had this subject on my mind for some time? I guess with Thanksgiving coming up, I've been meditating on real thanksgiving. In fact, I wrote a poem about my feelings.

LEADER—Really? Would you read it for us,————?

HOSTESS—I thought you'd never ask me! *(She goes to a table and takes poem from between the pages of a book.)* Here it is—My debut as a poet! All kidding aside, this is how I really feel about the subject. I call it:

"Two-Way Street"

My God, You've given so very much to me.
   Dare I ask You, Lord, for more—just one more thing?
A grateful heart is what I most desire.
   Not thankful only when my heart can sing,
As if Your blessings had good days and bad,
As if You shut them off when I feel sad.

I want to give You, God, a grateful heart
   Whose every pulsebeat is a note of praise,
Not measuring Your love by what I have,
   Or by the sun or rain or lonely days.

But let me wholly, totally respond.
Oh, let me, God, just stop in life's wild race
To give You true thanksgiving from my heart,
A daily heart response to Your great grace!

1st Speaker—Oh, ———, that was beautiful! Wasn't that good, ladies? That's the kind of thanks I want to give God. We have been given so much in Jesus Christ that if we were destitute we should still be grateful!

2nd Speaker—I think gratefulness is something that we need to practice. We need to teach our children to be thankful for small favors. We all need to cultivate the "thank you" habit, to each other, and certainly to God.

4th Speaker—I'd like a copy of your poem, ———. I want to hang it over my sink as a reminder.

5th Speaker—I want one, too, Julie. I really don't think we're ungrateful. Just forgetful. I need to be nudged once in a while.

6th Speaker *(to leader)*— ———, I'm glad you brought up this subject. This has been a good Thanksgiving reminder. It's been so helpful to me.

Leader—Thank you. It's been a help to me, too, and besides we got a lot of work done and had a beautiful lunch. Isn't God good? Besides all of the big things God does for us, He adds these little every-day favors that make us love Him all the more.

Hostess—I'm so glad all of you could be here. Thank you so much for coming. I thank God for each one of you dear Christian friends. I'm going to share our conversation with my family.

Other ladies *(ad lib)*—Me, too! Thanks, ———. Thanks for everything, etc. *(Exit.)*

A Thanksgiving Litany

By Grace Richie

Leader—We give Thee thanks, O Lord, for the freedom we enjoy in this land;

Response—May we never take these freedoms for granted or abuse them.

Leader—Thank You, Lord, for those who work in fields and factories to provide our food.

Response—And forgive us, Lord, for ever complaining when so many of Your children are hungry.

Leader—Thank You, Lord, for comfortable homes, and for the energy and opportunity to work and provide for our families.

Response—And thank You for humor and laughter that help to lighten the burden of our daily problems.

Leader—Thank You, Lord, for friends who stand by us no matter what happens.

Response—And for the courage and patience You provide in times of pain and tragedy.

Leader—Thank You, Lord, for voices to speak and sing, for ears to hear and minds to reason and think.

Response—And thank You for the ability to learn new things, and for willingness to accept needed change.

All—We praise You, Lord, for all of life, and thank You most of all for Your Son who came to give us the life more abundant. In His name we offer You our thanksgiving. Amen.

The Table Blessing

By Grace Richie

Scene—Dining room in a home, family seated at the table

Characters—Mother, Father, Son, and Daughter

FATHER—Son, would you ask the blessing please?

SON—But this isn't Thanksgiving!

DAUGHTER—Yeah, Thanksgiving's still a week away.

MOTHER—Well, we should thank God for our blessings every day, not just at Thanksgiving.

SON—Okay. *(hurried)* Thank You, God, for this food. Amen. *(He reaches for the potatoes almost before he says "Amen," and says:)* Pass the gravy.

FATHER—Hold on a minute there, young man. Don't be so grabby, and what about a please with that "pass the gravy"?

SON—Uh, sorry. Please pass the gravy.

MOTHER—By the way, do you children know when Thanksgiving originated?

SON—Sure. It was invented by the Pilgrims in A.D. 1620, and they invited the Indians to come and have dinner with them.

FATHER—Well, it's true the Pilgrims observed Thanksgiving and invited the Indians to share their meal, but they did not invent it.

DAUGHTER—They didn't? Then who did?

FATHER—You remember, don't you, that the Pilgrims came from England?

CHILDREN—Yes.

FATHER—Well, they had observed an annual celebration day of Thanksgiving in their native England for all of God's bounty and especially for the harvest. They celebrated on September 29, not in November (October) as we do. It was known as "Michaelmas" because on the church calendar it was listed as "The Feast of St. Michael and All Angels." It was a very big religious holiday.

SON—Did they have turkey for dinner, too?

MOTHER—No, they had roast goose. The Pilgrims had turkey because they found wild turkey while they were hunting for goose.

DAUGHTER—I'm glad it's turkey now. I don't think I'd like goose.

SON—How do you know? We've never even tasted goose, have we, Mom?

MOTHER—No, but maybe we should sometime.

FATHER—Did you know that not even Michaelmas in England was the beginning of Thanksgiving?

SON—It wasn't?

FATHER—No, the celebration goes back farther than that, because a "Feast of St. Martin of Tours" was a major holiday in western Europe in the Middle Ages. It was celebrated on November 11, and people went to mass, held parades, and played games, finishing with a festive dinner with—Guess what?

DAUGHTER—Roast goose?

MOTHER—Yes, roast goose! And because St. Martin's Day came after the harvests were in, it was known as a day of thanksgiving.

FATHER—And even that wasn't the real beginning of Thanksgiving!

SON—Hey, this is fun! We're tracing Thanksgiving's roots! *(Everyone laughs.)*

FATHER—In a way, that's exactly what we're doing. The very first Thanksgiving was celebrated long before the Christian Church came into being.

DAUGHTER—How come?

FATHER—I'll show you. Where's the Bible? *(Daughter goes to nearby stand and gets a Bible which she hands to her father.)* Let's see now, the first Thanksgiving is described in the Book of Leviticus, chapter 23. *(Hunts a bit.)* Here it is in verses 39-41. *(Reads aloud.)* You see, that was a thanksgiving for harvest, called the Feast of the Tabernacles.

SON—Why was it called that?

MOTHER—Because it was to be kept as a remembrance by the Israelites of the big tent they worshipped in while traveling in the wilderness. It was called a tabernacle. You remember that from your Sunday School lessons, don't you, when they escaped with God's help from Egypt, and wandered so long in the desert?

DAUGHTER—Oh, yeah! And God fed them manna!

SON—How long ago was that, Dad?

FATHER—About 3,200 years ago!

CHILDREN—Wow!

MOTHER—Now let's go back to why we decided to give thanks for our food every day, and not just on Thanksgiving. Can you tell me why we say a table blessing?

DAUGHTER—To thank God for our food.

FATHER—Yes, and the Bible says we're to be thankful all the time, not just at Thanksgiving, when we have a big turkey and special meal.

SON—Does that mean we should say thank You to God for every meal?

FATHER—Yes, it does, and that's what we're going to do from now on.

The Thank-You Bug

A skit by Steve Tippett

Players—
- MOTHER
- FATHER
- STEVE
- DOUG
- JEFF
- KRISTIN

The "Thank-you" Bug: dressed like a ladybug, carrying a magic wand.

OPENING SCENE—The breakfast table

MOTHER—Hurry up, kids. It's getting late! Honey, you'll miss your train!

FATHER—Coming! Hey, Hon, have you seen my striped tie? Oh, here it is.

STEVE—Ugh—oatmeal again?

JEFF—I'm sick of that stuff!

DOUG—Me, too!

KRISTIN—Right!

MOTHER—Now let's not be difficult. It's good for you. You need a good breakfast to think well in school.
(Father enters and sits down. Thank-you bug slips in, unnoticed.)

FATHER—Good morning *(pulls chair out)*. Don't tell me we're having *(bug touches him)* Oh, we're having oatmeal again. Well, let's thank the Lord for our food. *(prays)* Thank You, Lord, for a restful night. Be with us today and bring us home safely. Thank You now for our food. In Jesus' name, Amen. *(Family starts eating.)*

JEFF—Oh, no!

KRISTIN—What's the matter?

JEFF—I forgot to do my history assignment. It's due today, too. I hate school—it's a big *(bug touch; pause)* Well, I guess school's okay. If I didn't go, I'd grow up stupid. *(Pause)* Hey! That's true! But I wonder what made me say that?

MOTHER *(to husband)*—Dave, do you know how many times Margaret has called me this week? Four times! And when she gets on the phone she just *(bug touch)*—Well, I'm really glad Margaret does call me. I think I'm the only friend she has. She has so many problems to talk about.

JEFF—Can I have the toast, please? *(Mother passes it.)* And the jelly. Is that the only kind we . . . *(bug touch—pause)* I guess I should be thankful I've got jelly at all. My friend Billy says he sometimes gets only a glass of milk for breakfast, because his family is so poor.

STEVE—Hey, Dad, my allowance isn't doing the . . . *(bug touch)*

FATHER—What's that?

STEVE—Oh, never mind. I forgot what I was going to say. Well, not really. I was thinking about more allowance, but really, I'm making it all right, and I think I have a lead on a job.

FATHER—You know, I'm really disgusted at how much money is taken out of my paycheck for taxes. There ought to be *(bug touch—pause)* some thankfulness on my part, though. After all, if we didn't pay taxes there'd be no government, no police, no firemen, no roads, and a lot of other things. I guess I shouldn't gripe about it.

MOTHER—Well, finish up now, kids. You'd better pack up and go. The bus will be here in three minutes.

CHILDREN *(leaving)*—Bye, Mom! So long! Bye Mom!

FATHER—Well, dear *(she straightens tie)*—I'll see you around six. *(Kiss)* I hope that old boss of mine doesn't have any dumb jobs for me to do today. Boy, is he a pain in the *(bug touch—pause)*. You know, my boss may be pushy, but I really do like my job. Hey, what's going on around here? Everybody seems to stop in the middle of what they're saying. I wonder why? Well, see you tonight.

MOTHER—Bye. *(Father exits. Phone rings, and she carries out dishes as she goes to answer it.)*

SECOND SCENE—Sign held up "Dinner time." Mother enters to set the table.

MOTHER—Come and get it! Dinner's ready! Don't let it get cold. *(Family enters one or two at a time. Settle down and start serving.)*

STEVE—Boy, am I hungry! I could eat the table.

JEFF—Yeah, and Mom's spaghetti's tops! *(They all start eating. Bug touches Father.)*

FATHER—Wait—we forgot to say grace. It's your turn, Doug.

DOUG *(prays child's prayer)*

FATHER—Well, how did everything go today, kids?

STEVE—Okay.

JEFF—Fine.

DOUG—Yeah.

KRISTIN—Uh-huh.

FATHER—Is that all? *(Bug giggles and touches Kristin)*

KRISTIN—I had a nice day. *(Bug touches Doug.)*

DOUG—I did, too. I'm glad I've got so many friends and such a nice teacher. *(Bug touches Jeff)*

JEFF—I'm glad my teacher didn't yell at me for not having my homework done. He told me to hand in my assignment tomorrow. I didn't think he'd take it late, but he is. *(Bug touches Steve)*

STEVE—I had a good day, too. And it sure is great to come home to a nice family and good meal. *(Bug touches Mother)*

MOTHER—I'm glad Margaret called today. I just listened, but evidently she felt better after sharing with me.

FATHER—Everybody's acting so strange around here today, even me. And you know what? I like us this way!

MOTHER—I know what you mean! You'd think there was a Thank-you bug around!

STEVE—Ah, Mom! You're weird!